Advent and Christmas with Saint Joseph

Advent and Christmas with
Saint Joseph

Edited by Dr. Mary Amore

Our Sunday Visitor
Huntington, Indiana

Nihil Obstat
Msgr. Michael Heintz, Ph.D.
Censor Librorum

Imprimatur
✠ Kevin C. Rhoades
Bishop of Fort Wayne-South Bend
February 14, 2022

The *Nihil Obstat* and *Imprimatur* are official declarations that a book is free from doctrinal or moral error. It is not implied that those who have granted the *Nihil Obstat* and *Imprimatur* agree with the contents, opinions, or statements expressed.

Except where noted, the Scripture citations used in this work are taken from the *Revised Standard Version of the Bible — Second Catholic Edition* (Ignatius Edition), copyright © 1965, 1966, 2006 National Council of the Churches of Christ in the United States of America. Used by permission. All rights reserved.

Every reasonable effort has been made to determine copyright holders of excerpted materials and to secure permissions as needed. If any copyrighted materials have been inadvertently used in this work without proper credit being given in one form or another, please notify Our Sunday Visitor in writing so that future printings of this work may be corrected accordingly.

Copyright © 2022 by Mayslake Ministries

27 26 25 24 23 22   1 2 3 4 5 6 7 8 9

All rights reserved. With the exception of short excerpts for critical reviews, no part of this work may be reproduced or transmitted in any form or by any means whatsoever without permission from the publisher. For more information, visit: www.osv.com/permissions.

Our Sunday Visitor Publishing Division
Our Sunday Visitor, Inc.
200 Noll Plaza
Huntington, IN 46750
www.osv.com
1-800-348-2440

ISBN: 978-1-63966-015-5 (Inventory No. T2753)
1. RELIGION—Holidays—Christmas & Advent.
2. RELIGION—Christianity—Saints & Sainthood.
3. RELIGION—Christianity—Catholic.

LCCN: 2022933183

Cover and interior design: Lindsey Riesen
Cover art: AdobeStock

PRINTED IN THE UNITED STATES OF AMERICA

~ FAITHFULNESS ~

First Sunday of Advent

I am the way, and the truth, and the life; no one comes to the Father, but by me. — John 14:6

Advent is a challenging time of the year for me. I struggle to strike the right balance between spending quiet time in prayerful preparation for Christmas and enjoying all the trappings of holiday activities like parties and gift giving. In the depths of my heart, however, the Lord continues to call me. I know that the only way to find the truth and life of this season is to seek it in prayerful silence, contemplating the miracle of the Christ child.

The Lord chose Saint Joseph to guard his truth in this world. Joseph was a man of God and he dedicated his entire life to keeping his family safe so the world would eventually come to know and love Jesus. This Advent season, let us turn to Saint Joseph to help us open our eyes that we may truly experience Jesus as the way, the truth, and the life.

— Gina Sannasardo

IN WHAT WAYS do you strive to be faithful to the truth?

Prayer: Saint Joseph teach me, by your loving example, to depend upon God for all things, that I may be a witness to the Truth of Christ in this season. Amen.

First Week of Advent, Monday

Where you go I will go, and where you lodge I will lodge;
your people shall be my people, and your God my God.
— Ruth 1:16

At first, Joseph struggled with the news of Mary's pregnancy, and he was going to divorce her quietly because he was loyal to Mary and wanted to protect her. After the angel told Joseph not to be afraid, he took Mary into his home.

Joseph's faithfulness to Mary reminds me of my own marriage. My husband's name is Joseph (Mary and Joseph!), and this year marks our forty-fifth anniversary. In good times and bad, we have remained faithful to one another, rooted in love for God and commitment to each other.

Joseph was steadfast in his commitment to love and care for Mary and Jesus. Wherever their journey took them in life, Joseph kept his holy family safe from harm. The life of Joseph as husband and father shows how important faithfulness is in relationships.

— Dr. Mary Amore

REFLECT ON THE RELATIONSHIPS in your life. Do you struggle with being faithful? Seek Saint Joseph's help to be faithful and loyal in your dealings with others.

Prayer: Saint Joseph, husband of Mary and father of Jesus, help me to deepen my faithfulness to God and to those in my family. Amen.

First Week of Advent, Tuesday

His master said to him, "Well done, good and faithful servant; you have been faithful over a little, I will set you over much." — Matthew 25:21

In Scripture, we hear that Joseph was a righteous man, and in the short time that we encounter him we see clearly that he was. Joseph did all that God asked of him — whether he was told not to divorce Mary, or to travel to Egypt and back with his family, he promptly took action.

Not only was Joseph faithful to God, but he was also faithful to the promises he made to Mary and Jesus. He actively supported and protected them. Joseph's faithfulness is why God chose him to be Jesus' earthly father. Joseph had proven his fidelity; therefore, God made him the guardian of Our Lord and Savior. He was given the awesome responsibility of not only protecting Jesus but teaching and guiding him in his early life. Joseph was faithful both in his love for God and in his love for those entrusted to his care.

— Maria Pusateri

WHAT ABOUT US? Are we faithful to the responsibilities we have been given? When called upon, do we promptly do what God asks?

Prayer: Saint Joseph, help me to be faithful so that one day I may hear, "Well done my good and faithful servant." Amen.

First Week of Advent, Wednesday

*I believe that I shall see the goodness of the LORD
in the land of the living! — Psalm 27:13*

I knew a man who went to a church with a burden on his heart. He went to Mass hoping for a message, guidance or comfort. After the homily, the man picked up a missalette and read: "I shall see the goodness of the Lord." Immediately, he experienced comfort and peace. His faith in God did not disappoint.

For his entire life, Joseph lived as a pious and faithful Israelite. He faithfully attended synagogue and was guided by Scripture, including the psalms. His life was challenged by the news that Mary was with child. What was he to do? Surely he sought God in prayer each day in this impossible situation. Joseph experienced the goodness of the Lord when his prayers were answered through the message of an angel.

The life of Joseph challenges us to believe in God's goodness no matter how difficult the situation may be. If we remain faithful to God, as Joseph did, we will discover his goodness in our life.

— Larry Dreffein, OFM

ASK SAINT JOSEPH to help you to discover the goodness of the Lord in your daily challenges.

Prayer: Faithful Joseph, help me to believe that in my times of challenge and struggle you will assist me in seeing the goodness that these difficulties will bring to my life. Amen.

First Week of Advent, Thursday

And her husband Joseph, being a just man and unwilling to put her to shame, resolved to send her away quietly.
— *Matthew 1:19*

Faithfulness is the quality of being steadfast, reliant, faithful, unfailing, and remaining loyal no matter the circumstance or cost. It is not duty; it is not exhibition. It is defining one's life in the context of other.

According to the laws and customs of their day, Joseph and Mary's betrothal meant they were already considered husband and wife, with all the full legal rights that marriage would seal. The contractual agreements had been reached, and the consents had been given. So you can imagine the crisis that Mary's announcement brought. The law gave Joseph rights and authority, but Joseph chose faithfulness instead, staying true to his word, no matter the circumstance or the cost to himself.

Faithfulness is just one of God's unchanging attributes. God always does what he promises, always keeps his word to us. And it is this promise of faithfulness that is the foundation of our hope.

— Colleen Case

WHERE HAVE YOU SEEN God's faithfulness in your life? Where do you need God's faithfulness?

Prayer: Blessed Saint Joseph, pray for me, that I may come to know the faithfulness of God, our Father. Amen.

First Week of Advent, Friday

*You shall be careful to do therefore as the LORD your God
has commanded you; you shall not turn aside to the right
hand or to the left. You shall walk in all the way which the
LORD your God has commanded you, that you may live,
and that it may go well with you.*
— *Deuteronomy 5:32–33*

Saint Joseph's voice is silent in the Gospel. None of his words are recorded. Yet Joseph is certainly one of our greatest role models. His silence could never be understood as apathy because his actions spoke so boldly. He showed his faithfulness by allowing God to lead the way. He was a man who, regardless of any inner struggles he may have had, faithfully followed the promptings of the Spirit. Like Saint Joseph, we all face trials and inner struggles. Sometimes our own plans and expectations must change dramatically. Saint Joseph teaches us to trust God completely and with every detail of our lives.

— Lori Bertucci-Thibeau

TAKE SOME TIME with Saint Joseph and ask him to share with you how he was able to remain faithful and persevere even when exhausted. As you clear your mind and relax, listen for his encouragement and love.

Prayer: Saint Joseph, help me to listen and surrender. Show me how to become quiet and peaceful so I may better see God's will and follow it. Amen.

First Week of Advent, Saturday

Be still, and know that I am God. — *Psalm 46:10*

The times we stand on the uncertain threshold of the future are the times that test our faithfulness. Where do we turn when we face the unknown with the loss of a job, a move to a new home, retirement, an unexpected illness, or the effects of an unseen virus?

Joseph can be our guide to prepare us for faithfulness in uncertain times. We are told that Joseph was a righteous man, devout in the practice of his Jewish faith. His faithfulness brought him to daily prayer. As his prayer life deepened, so did his relationship with God. The guidance he received from God, though, did not come in words. It came in the silence of the night. Joseph moved beyond talking to God; he learned to listen in silence. Without silence, he would not have heard God speak. Silence prepares us to hear God's voice.

— JoAnne McElroy

HOW DO I KNOW whether I am being faithful to God or pursuing my own desires?

Prayer: Saint Joseph, faithful guide, teach me to open my heart to hear God's voice in silence. Amen.

~ OBEDIENCE ~

Second Sunday of Advent

Philip found Nathana-el, and said to him, "We have found him of whom Moses in the law and also the prophets wrote, Jesus of Nazareth, the son of Joseph."
— *John 1:45*

Saint Joseph was raised in the Mosaic law. He knew the ancient stories and, like Philip and Nathanael years later, he eagerly awaited the coming Messiah. Joseph probably did not anticipate that he would meet the long-awaited Messiah in his lifetime. Then everything changed.

I grew up knowing the story of Mary, Joseph, and Jesus. My parents, religious sisters, and priests all shared stories of faith with me. I remember that my grandmother had statues of Joseph and the Holy Family in her house; and I loved to play with Nativity scenes. These tangible objects made the Christmas stories come to life for me when I was young.

As I grew into adulthood, I experienced God's divine presence through faith-sharing, retreats, Mass, and the sacraments. I fell in love with God. This was not what I expected or planned. Everything changed.
— Sue Rooney

HAS THE TRUTH about Jesus come alive for me?

Prayer: Saint Joseph, inspire me to see the unexpected ways that the Messiah arrives as I eagerly await his coming at Christmas. Amen.

Second Week of Advent, Monday

But this command I gave them, "Obey my voice, and I will be your God, and you shall be my people; and walk in all the way that I command you, that it may be well with you." — Jeremiah 7:23

In my home office, there's an old wingback chair and a little oak table just large enough to hold my Bible, a couple of spiritual books, holy water, and an antique, wind-up pocket watch that still keeps perfect time. I've spent many hours in that chair trying to discern God's will for me.

When God reveals his will to us, he asks us to be obedient, and he always provides grace and courage to move forward. Obedience takes humility, but God promises he will "lift us up in due time" (1 Pt 5:6). For his entire life, Joseph humbly walked in the ways of the Lord. When God's will was revealed to him by an angel, I can only imagine the profound humility and courage it must have taken to obey God in those early days of Mary's pregnancy. He continued to remain open and obedient to God's will throughout Jesus' childhood, being a good and loving father and husband.

— Mary Lally

WHAT IS GOD revealing about his will for your life today?

Prayer: Saint Joseph, most obedient, pray for us! Amen.

Second Week of Advent, Tuesday

Make me to know your ways, O Lord;
teach me your paths. — Psalm 25:4

What was life like for Joseph of Nazareth? By all accounts, he was a good man who lived a discreet life as a carpenter and worked hard providing for his family. As a child and then a young man, he would have seen his faith through youthful eyes — its truth handed down to him from his parents and the local Rabbi. Joseph would have been obedient to the Jewish laws which made clear what is right and wrong, what is allowed and forbidden.

Then life happened. What did Joseph experience when the law given to Moses by God seemed to conflict with what God was asking of him? One can almost hear the rumbling of his imagination. "It doesn't make sense. How can I be obedient to the Lord and disobedient to the law at the same time?" I picture Joseph taking time to navigate the contradictions and questions. At some point, though, God drew him into a deeper and more personal relationship. Joseph was attentive, listening to and obeying God's divine guidance.
— Joanne McElroy

Joseph was obedient to the inner guidance of God. To whom are you obedient?

Prayer: Obedient Joseph, teach me how to listen and open my heart to the inspirations of divine guidance. Amen.

Second Week of Advent, Wednesday

Keep the charge of the LORD your God, walking in his ways and keeping his statues, his commandments, his ordinances, and his testimonies, as it is written in the law of Moses. — 1 Kings 2:3

Joseph was a devout Jew and observed the law of Moses. But more than being obedient to the law, Joseph was obedient to God.

When our kids were young, my husband and I took a parenting class and learned how important it was to teach our children to obey the first time an instruction was given. We were not perfect teaching it, and they were not perfect practicing it. But when it came to the important things, they obeyed — no questions asked. They obeyed because they trusted that we loved them and knew what was best for them.

Joseph obeyed God because he trusted him. Even when things did not make sense, Joseph knew that God loved him. He understood that God knew what was best for him and his family. No questions asked.

— Denine Chambers

IS THERE A SITUATION where God is calling you to walk in obedience to him? Turn to the example of Saint Joseph for guidance.

Prayer: Saint Joseph, help me to be obedient as you were in all situations. Amen.

Second Week of Advent, Thursday

Now therefore, if you will obey my voice and keep my covenant, you shall be my own possession among all peoples.
— *Exodus 19:5*

Saint Joseph offers us an example of how to live obediently and to love the Lord faithfully even when life is complicated. When Joseph initially heard of Mary's pregnancy, he struggled, and he prayed to God that he would do the right and just thing for Mary in this precarious situation.

There are times when I find myself asking, "What is the right thing to do?" More often than not, there is no easy answer, nor is the solution clearly marked out on my journey of faith.

We can turn to Saint Joseph for help to lead and guide us when we are unclear of the path ahead. He is our spiritual father, and he is here to help us obey the voice of our God.

— Deacon Jerry Souta

RECALL A TIME when you were unsure of what the "right thing" was. Where did you turn for an answer? Today, invite Saint Joseph into your life to lead and guide your steps that you may faithfully follow the ways of the Lord.

Prayer: Saint Joseph, teach me how to obey so that my life may bear great fruit for the kingdom of God. Amen.

Second Week of Advent, Friday

When Joseph woke from sleep, he did as the angel of the Lord commanded him; he took his wife. — *Matthew 1:24*

While I have always known of Saint Joseph's obedience to God, it was not until I became a parent that I marveled at his quiet and humble obedience. Never do we read in the New Testament that Saint Joseph stood up and proclaimed, "Look at me! Aren't I amazing? Without me, none of this would have happened!"

As much as I chuckle at the thought, I recall a few times when I craved some recognition for the sacrifices I had made for my family. Joseph did not. Instead, he displayed quiet obedience by trusting God at great expense. He did not dwell on whether he would be recognized or respected by others. He did not announce his sacrifices from the mountaintops or tell others, hoping that his actions would earn him a reputation for holiness. It was enough for him to carry out the will of God in quiet obedience. Whatever it is that makes us yearn for attention can decrease if we follow Saint Joseph's example.

— Meg Bucaro

WHAT OR WHO are you struggling to obey today? Seek the help of Saint Joseph in your endeavor.

Prayer: Saint Joseph, please help me to obey God's will for me today without attention or recognition. Amen.

Second Week of Advent, Saturday

But he said, "Blessed rather are those who hear the word of God and keep it!"
Luke 11:28

To practice obedience, we must learn the art of listening. Sacred listening formed Joseph's heart. Joseph and Mary are called holy because they heard the word of God, received it into their hearts, and then responded. Joseph responded to God with actions. His fiat was first given when the angel came to him in a dream. Joseph awoke and did as the angel instructed.

God also spoke through the law and the prophets. Joseph was a faithful Jew, and he obediently carried out the precepts of the law prescribed in his duties as a loving husband and father. The circumcision, the presentation in the Temple, the naming of Jesus: These were all the duties of the Jewish father.

In order to obey God's word, we must learn to be quiet and listen, then consider how we might act. By listening in prayer, we can learn to express our own *fiat* — that is, "let it be done." Saint Joseph is here to help us.

— Sr. Mary McNulty

Is THERE SPACE in your life to listen and respond?

Prayer: Saint Joseph, you awoke and did as the angel instructed. Instruct my heart to hear God's word and respond to God's will in my life. Amen.

~ TENDERNESS ~

Third Sunday of Advent

*He heals the brokenhearted,
and binds up their wounds. — Psalm 147:3*

I imagine there were many times where Joseph comforted Jesus in his arms as he was growing up. He surely kissed the skinned knee of his little boy when he stumbled on uneven stones learning how to walk, and bandaged injuries that occurred while learning the trade of carpentry. At the end of the day, as was the custom, Joseph helped Jesus practice their faith, praying together to the God of Abraham, Isaac, and Jacob. We tend to forget this human side of Joseph because there are no written records which describe the home life of the Holy Family.

Today, families are in crisis, and many do not experience a father's tenderness. Who will heal the brokenhearted? Who will bind up their wounds? Saint Joseph can help us restore love and tenderness in our families. As the beloved foster father of Jesus, he is waiting for us to turn to him for guidance in raising our families with Jesus at the center.

— Dr. Mary Amore

TODAY, ASK SAINT JOSEPH to help you treat others with tenderness and compassion.

Prayer: Saint Joseph, you raised Jesus with tenderness. Help me to follow your example that I may be gentle in my dealings with others. Amen.

Third Week of Advent, Monday

Come, my beloved,
let us go forth into the fields,
and lodge in the villages. — Song of Solomon 7:11

One can only imagine what Joseph felt when he had to make a long journey to Bethlehem near the end of Mary's pregnancy. As a faithful man of God, Joseph lovingly cared for his family with great tenderness. His tenderness is on display when there is no room at the inn, and they must spend the night in the fields surrounded by animals. A stable was the best he could do. That night, it became a place of extraordinary tenderness.

The life of Saint Joseph reminds us that life is not always easy, and no matter how much we prepare, things may not go as planned. Joseph is here to walk with us. He invites us to be loving and caring individuals and to treat one another with the tenderness that can make something good of even the worst situation.
— Larry Dreffein, OFM

ARE THERE PEOPLE in your life that you treat harshly? Ask Saint Joseph to help you to be more tender in your dealings with your family and friends.

Prayer: Joseph, help me to be a source of tenderness to my family, my friends, and the people I meet in my life's journey. May I see the needs of others and tenderly address them. Amen.

Third Week of Advent, Tuesday

The LORD is my shepherd, I shall not want;
he makes me lie down in green pastures.
He leads me beside still waters;
he restores my soul. — Psalm 23:1–3

Joseph was familiar with this psalm and prayed to God, his Shepherd, to lead and guide him. How Joseph must have struggled when he heard of Mary's pregnancy. He must have wondered where he would find restful waters in this situation. But he knew God was there to lead him, that the Lord would respond with tenderness. Joseph's life clearly reminds us that we are to turn to God in all situations — especially the most painful and challenging experiences. The Lord is our Shepherd, too, and he will tenderly lead us and refresh our weary souls. Let us seek the help of Saint Joseph when we are in crisis and ask him to lead us to the tenderness of our loving God.

— Larry Dreffein, OFM

HOW DO I RESPOND to unexpected situations and disruptions in my own life? Do I turn to God for direction and guidance? Let us ask Saint Joseph to help us follow the pathways that lead us to the Lord.

Prayer: Joseph, husband of Mary and foster father of Jesus, help me to be tender and kind to others when unexpected changes and challenges occur. In times of trouble, lead me to the peaceful waters that refresh my soul. Amen.

Third Week of Advent, Wednesday

As a father pities his children,
so the LORD pities those who fear him. — *Psalm 103:13*

In Saint Joseph, we discover a daily discreet and hidden presence, a support and a guide in times of trouble. Saint Joseph reminds us that those who go unnoticed, who seem hidden in the shadows, quietly doing their part, often play an incomparable role in the lives of others and even in history. The greatness of Saint Joseph is mostly hidden; he was a kind and loving spouse to Mary and father to Jesus.

Saint Joseph stood at the crossroads of the Old and New Testaments. The psalms were Joseph's prayer book, memorized and taught to Jesus so he, too, would be soaked in the tender love and constancy of God. Like God, Joseph approached everything with a spirit of kindness, compassion, and great tenderness. Let us turn to Saint Joseph that he may intercede for us as we pray for a kind and open heart, and a tenderness of soul.

— Dr. Jill Bates

RECALL A TIME when you tenderly responded with love to those in need.

Prayer: Saint Joseph, father of Jesus and spouse of Mary, I ask for your support in my daily life. Show me how to connect with others lovingly and tenderly. Amen.

Third Week of Advent, Thursday

He will feed his flock like a shepherd,
he will gather the lambs in his arms. — *Isaiah 40:11*

Amazing happenings — the proclamation of angels, visits by shepherds and kings from the East — surrounded the birth of Jesus. It was a lot for the Holy Family to take in. Scripture tells us that Mary "kept all these things in her heart." Surely, Joseph, too, reflected on Jesus' birth.

Joseph brought his firstborn child to be presented to God in the Temple. For Joseph this was a sacred duty, exercised with the tenderness of a loving father. The privilege of naming Jesus also belonged to Joseph. One can imagine that, as a new father, he gathered his son in his arms with tenderness and amazement, imagining what this child's life would be. He invites us to reflect on our own lives and the ways we experience the tender mercies of God as we go about our daily duties: taking care of our families, interacting with coworkers, and caring for those less fortunate. Joseph can help us recognize the tenderness of God.

— Sr. Mary McNulty

How have you experienced the tender love of God in your life? How have you shared it?

Prayer: Saint Joseph, remind me of the tender love of God, embrace me, and keep me safe. Amen.

Third Week of Advent, Friday

One thing have I asked of the LORD …
that I may dwell in the house of the LORD
all the days of my life,
to behold the beauty of the LORD,
and to inquire in his temple. — Psalm 27:4

Parents know the delight of gazing at their newborn child and seeing part of themselves reflecting back at them. Imagine Joseph gazing upon the beauty of his newborn son, Jesus. Does he see Mary's features? Does he see the face of God? I picture Joseph holding his infant son and gazing upon him with tenderness. Jesus, Love Incarnate! Joseph is lovingly looking upon the face of God, as God lovingly looks at the face of Joseph. Can you see the tenderness and holiness of this moment? When I place myself in this scene, my heart overflows with love and joy as I gaze at the Lord's beauty and feel him looking back at me. As I look at the infant Jesus, he gazes upon me as his beautiful beloved daughter, which never leaves me.

— Denine Chambers

Set aside a few moments of quiet. Imagine looking into Jesus' eyes, as he gazes at you with an unending love. What arises in your heart?

Prayer: Saint Joseph, help me to remember to keep my eyes upon Jesus. Amen.

Third Week of Advent, Saturday

He will carry them in his bosom,
and gently lead those that are with young.
— Isaiah 40:11

I once came across a beautiful picture of the Holy Family, unlike any I had seen before. Saint Joseph was in the foreground, cradling baby Jesus in his arms, looking down at him tenderly. In the background, Mary lay sleeping. I remember thinking how wonderful it was to see an image of Joseph as a husband and father, allowing Mary to sleep while he cared for Jesus.

The Holy Family was, in many ways, a family just like ours. As the head of the household, it was Joseph's responsibility to provide for Mary and Jesus. Furnishing food and shelter for his family was essential, but Joseph also loved and supported Mary and Jesus in all of their needs. Joseph tenderly cared for his family.
— Maria Pusateri

Is THERE SOMEONE in your life who needs some tenderness? Try walking with them today.

Prayer: Saint Joseph, thank you for the tender love that you showed to Mary and Jesus. Teach me how to show tenderness to others as you did. Amen.

~ COURAGE ~

Fourth Sunday of Advent

What then shall we say to this? If God is for us, who can be against us? — Romans 8:31

Saint Joseph demonstrated the virtue and value of courage. Fortified by his faith in God, he was able to endure all things.

We all know how difficult it can be to face danger, rejection, or disappointment. When we walk with Joseph, we learn that courage is tested in the midst of crisis; it is developed in difficult situations. We can take comfort knowing that God is not against us, but for us. Living courageously in truth and with God is exactly what Saint Joseph models for us. This is the courage that inspires as well as empowers us. The more we trust in God, the more we grow not only in the virtue of courage but all the virtues. We tap into the life of faith in which God bathes us in grace and is with us — and for us — at every turn.

— Lori Bertucci-Thibeau

INVITE SAINT JOSEPH to help you overcome a spirit of fear and to bring you to a place of security that only courageously living can bring.

Prayer: Saint Joseph, strengthen my faith when I am most afraid. Inspire me to be more like you and face each day's challenges with courage because I know that God is for me. Amen.

Fourth Week of Advent, Monday

An angel of the Lord appeared to him in a dream, saying, "Joseph, son of David, do not fear to take Mary your wife." — Matthew 1:20

Courage is an attribute often overlooked when we think of Joseph, even though his role in God's plan called for courage from the very beginning. Jewish life had strict rules. Mary's pregnancy prior to the completion of the marriage process brought shame and dishonor not only to her, but to Joseph as well. He could have maintained his own social status and honor by subjecting her to the law or divorcing her quietly. Joseph knew that God often calls us out of our comfort zones; following his will takes courage. It took courage for Joseph to follow the angel's instructions and continue with the marriage as planned. By doing God's will, he went against the customs, rituals, and expectations of his day.

— Bob Frazee

WE ARE CHALLENGED to follow Joseph's example. Are there cultural values you accept without any reflection? How often are you faced with the choice of going along with the group or giving in to peer pressure when you know those things are opposed to God's will? Can you be courageous then?

Prayer: Beloved Saint Joseph, role model of courage, pray for us.

Fourth Week of Advent, Tuesday

God is our refuge and strength,
a very present help in trouble. — Psalm 46:1

As a man of God, Joseph stayed out of trouble. He followed the laws of his time and was a good neighbor and friend. In order for Joseph to comply with Caesar's census, he had to return to his birthplace, Bethlehem, with Mary to be counted. Joseph had the courage to do what was expected of him, and even though Mary was about to give birth, they traveled together to Bethlehem. The journey that Mary and Joseph took was arduous, yet Joseph prevailed: He courageously protected Mary and her newborn son.

Joseph's courage came from his deep faith in God, in whom he found refuge and strength. Joseph obeyed civil authorities that imposed rules and regulations that were at times unjust. But Joseph had the courage to follow the laws of the land and the Law of the Lord. Saint Joseph can help us be good citizens of the world, and good citizens of God's kingdom.

— Alice Smith

CONSIDER THE WAYS that Saint Joseph's life can help you to courageously follow God in the midst of a culture of sin and death.

Prayer: Saint Joseph, provide the courage I need to assess my duties as a good citizen and a faithful follower of Christ. Amen.

Fourth Week of Advent, Wednesday

When I am afraid,
I put my trust in you.
In God, whose word I praise,
in God I trust without a fear. — Psalm 56:3–4

As a faithful Jewish man, Joseph was familiar with this Scripture and probably prayed it frequently. This had an impact on his relationship with God. Joseph believed in God's faithfulness, and this awareness helped Joseph to be victorious over his fears and doubts. Joseph turned to the Lord for strength and courage, especially when he was afraid.

We live in a troubled world where many of us are anxious and fearful. But if we let fear and anxiety rule our lives, we will never be victorious over the sin of this world. Instead, we can follow in the footsteps of Joseph, who sought the Lord's help and strength in dealing with the adversities of life.

— Dr. Mary Amore

REFLECT ON THE SITUATIONS in your life that are causing you fear and anxiety. How does the knowledge that God is trustworthy help you to overcome your feelings?

Prayer: Saint Joseph, you are a model of spiritual courage for me. Help me to follow your example that I may faithfully turn to the Lord for strength to overcome the difficulties of life. Amen.

Fourth Week of Advent, Thursday

Be watchful, stand firm in your faith, be courageous, be strong. — 1 Corinthians 16:13

Each day I wake up to the ordinariness of life. Routine activities fill my days: preparing meals, caring for my family, work, and volunteering, with little thought of courage. Yet courage is part of our daily life. We do not have to go far from home to be courageous, for we never know what this day will bring. We are courageous in the daily choices we make that touch our hearts deeply and lead us to action for the greater good.

Joseph modeled courage when he took upon himself all the challenges he faced in the early events of his life with Mary. He was courageous in taking a pregnant bride on a long journey, then fleeing with his family to a foreign country, and eventually returning home to Nazareth. Joseph faced fear each time he responded to God speaking to him; but Joseph overcame his fears by faith. We can overcome our fears as Joseph did, by trusting more deeply in God.

— Joanne McElroy

WHAT FEARS are you facing where God is asking you to be courageous?

Prayer: Saint Joseph, help me to face my fears, to be courageous and trust in the Lord. Amen.

Fourth Week of Advent, Friday

Be watchful, stand firm in your faith, be courageous, be strong. — *1 Corinthians 16:13*

It is clear that Joseph loved Mary and Jesus. From the moment that Joseph courageously took Mary into his home, Joseph assumed the responsibility of protecting Mary and her baby from all harm. Throughout his life, Joseph did not give in to fear or worry, but chose to place his complete trust in God. This gave him the unwavering courage to carry on his responsibilities as husband and father. Joseph stood firm in his faith in God; his life invites us to do the same.

Our world is a troubled place, and while we have no control over what happens in life, we do have control over how we respond to a situation or an event. We have the choice to place our trust in God. Let us turn to Saint Joseph and ask him for the courage to place our complete trust in the will of God that we, too, may stand firm in our faith.

— Carol Schubert

SOMEONE ONCE OBSERVED that it is impossible to have courage without first being afraid. What fear is your opportunity for courage today?

Prayer: Saint Joseph, help me to stand firm in my faith and be courageous in all that I do. Amen.

Fourth Week of Advent, Saturday

But you, take courage! Do not let your hands be weak, for
your work shall be rewarded. — 2 Chronicles 15:7

No one knows what Joseph was thinking or feeling on the night Jesus was born. Was he scared? Did he worry about being a good father? The Lord had called Joseph, and now he had to find the strength and courage to be what Mary and Jesus needed him to be. Mary carried the child in her womb and protected Jesus for nine months. Now Joseph is entrusted with caring for Mary and her child.

Ask any mom or dad, and they will tell you it takes courage to be a parent. Being responsible for the safety and well-being of an innocent child is not for the faint of heart. When our daughter was born, I watched my husband gently take her in his rough worker's hands as if she was glass. He held her with a quiet strength and a sense of courage, calming her little tears as she fell asleep.

— Lauren Nelson

How can the courage of Saint Joseph inspire you to take on the challenges God is placing before you today?

Prayer: Saint Joseph, your courage gives me strength to accept and face my fears. Help me to open my hands to God's plan for me. Amen.

~ LOVE AND ~
PROTECTION

December 24, Christmas Eve

Love is patient and kind. ... Love does not insist on its
own way; it is not irritable or resentful.
— *1 Corinthians 13:4–5*

One Christmas, I struggled to put together our daughters' dollhouse. With over one hundred plastic pieces, I sat on the floor angry with myself for saving the money to buy it. Sweaty, tired, and frustrated — but determined — I almost gave up. Our youngest sat down with me and said, "When I get mad because I can't do something, you tell me to ask for help." I looked at the two girls and said, "I need help." Suddenly, the project became fun. When done, I no longer looked at that pink monstrosity with anger and resentment. Yes, the stickers were crooked, and the door swung the wrong way, but we made it together with love.

We know Joseph as a carpenter, but in Greek, the word is tékton, which means craftsperson or master of the building trade. Before Jesus began his ministry, he was a tékton, too. Jesus used metaphors like "cornerstone" or "solid foundations" to explain God's kingdom to us. Perhaps those things reminded him of the love he shared with his foster father, Joseph.

— Lauren Nelson

Is THERE A situation you need help with?

Prayer: Saint Joseph, when I am irritated or resentful, help me to love. Amen.

December 25, Christmas Day

Blessed are the pure in heart, for they shall see God.
— Matthew 5:8

Like most mothers, when my children were born, I did not see them first. This privilege belonged to my husband. Something beautiful happens when a father holds his child for the first time, something that makes me think it might be the real meaning of love at first sight.

We can only speculate about who helped Mary deliver Jesus, but both infancy narratives agree that Joseph was present. While God chose Mary to conceive and bear his Son, God chose Joseph as well. It was his deep faith and purity of heart that enabled him to be the first to lay eyes on the miracle of that first Christmas night. Holding baby Jesus in his arms, Joseph's eyes beheld the purest form of love on earth. Surely, at that moment Joseph fell in love at first sight with Jesus.

— Lauren Nelson

WHEN DID YOU "see" or "hold" Jesus? How can you help someone else experience that today?

Prayer: Saint Joseph, help me to keep my heart pure in the love of Jesus. Open my eyes to see the Child Jesus in all people and to open the eyes of others to see Jesus in me. Amen.

December 26

And while they were there, the time came for her to be delivered. And she gave birth to her firstborn son and wrapped him in swaddling cloths, and laid him in a manger, because there was no place for them in the inn.
— Luke 2:6–7

Joseph was not a superhuman being in the true Christmas story. He was a humble man of faith, whose wife gave birth in less-than-ideal circumstances he could do little about. Yet, through all of this, Joseph's faith in God's plan never wavered. He remained steadfast in doing God's will. He allowed the truth to form him.

Like Joseph, we, too, encounter experiences in our lives that leave us disappointed, fearful, or afraid. What are we to do when our life seems chaotic? Let us look to Joseph, for in the face of unbelievable circumstances, Joseph clung to his faith in God. He did not question, nor did he try to understand what was going on; Joseph simply put his faith and trust in God, and he is here to help us do the same.

— Dr. Mary Amore

ASK SAINT JOSEPH to help you remain steadfast in your faith even in the face of difficulties.

Prayer: Saint Joseph, hold my hand and help me to live each day with the profound faith that you exemplified. Amen.

December 27

Greet one another with the kiss of love. Peace to all of you that are in Christ. — 1 Peter 5:14

Our firstborn son was minutes old when my husband lifted him out of my arms, cradled him, and gave him his first kiss. The depth of a father's love was palpable in this unforgettable and moving moment, which became a tradition at each child's birth. The "first kiss" was bigger than the three of us in those hospital rooms. It was the kiss, both of God the Father and of generations of our ancestral fathers and mothers, welcoming new life into the world.

God chose Joseph to shower Jesus with his love. God wanted Jesus to experience human love in a way that would prepare him for his ministry of mercy and compassion for all. As Joseph welcomed Jesus into the world with a kiss, he is inviting us to find God's fatherly love for us in the example of his life.

— Kathy Micheli

WHEN DID SOMEONE greet you in an extraordinarily moving way? Did you feel God's presence?

Prayer: Saint Joseph, I ask for your intercession for my prayer intentions today. Move my heart in love as you protect and guide me to live a life of mercy and compassion. Amen.

December 28, Holy Innocents

The name of the LORD is a strong tower;
the righteous man runs into it and is safe.
— *Proverbs 18:10*

As a man, Saint Joseph has many facets, but at the core of his character lies the fact that he was a father. We know the early stories: Joseph accepting fatherhood even before his marriage took place, thereby giving his child a family; being present as his son was born into this world; caring for his wife and infant son on the Flight to Egypt. One must wonder what it was like for Joseph as Jesus grew in wisdom and grace. What was it like to be an earthly father to such an exceptional child?

Protection can take many forms — keeping others safe from physical harm and emotional pain, offering guidance so that they can make the right decisions, teaching life skills so that they can protect themselves as they grow and go out into the world.

— Dr. Elizabeth McGovern

WHAT LESSONS would Saint Joseph have imparted that helped to shape Jesus and his understanding of the world around him? In what ways would he have protected Jesus and helped him grow?

Prayer: Saint Joseph, help me to protect and teach those I love so that they can go out in the world with faith in their own strengths and abilities. Amen.

December 29

I am my beloved's and my beloved is mine.
— Song of Solomon 6:3

From the moment Joseph took Mary into his home, he was steadfast in his love for Mary and Our Lord. Together they built a life centered on their love for God and each other. Though their days were filled with prayer, work, service, laughter, and tears, Joseph and Mary remained each other's biggest support and constant beloved. They upheld each other in every circumstance, praising God for all their blessings. Their mutual love for God and one another provided the foundation for Jesus to grow into his mission.

As a Catholic couple, my husband is my priority, and I am his. We both hold our mutual love for God above our relationships. Christian marriage comes with the important responsibility of helping your spouse get to heaven. Love of God and love of spouse is the heart of a Christian marriage. We belong to each other because we belong to God. We love because we are also beloved.

— Amy Bovie

As the beloved, how do you show your love for God and others daily?

Prayer: Saint Joseph, please help heal broken marriages and restore the sanctity of marriage and family to the elevation of God's design. Amen.

December 30

*Truly, I say to you, this poor widow has put in more than
all those who are contributing to the treasury. For they all
contributed out of their abundance; but she out of her pov-
erty has put in everything she had, her whole living.*
— Mark 12:43–44

Sometimes it's much easier to avoid someone or
turn away than it is to love them. There are a hundred
excuses not to extend myself, not to give, not to be
loving. When I sit in solitude before the Lord, however, I am reminded of what love requires. I realize
that sometimes my desire to be right is an obstacle
to love. I recall that love speaks louder in action than
it does in words and that more blessings come from
giving than from receiving.

Through prayer, I come to understand that the life
of Joseph was one of quiet loving action as he stood
by Mary, supporting, protecting, and guiding her —
not with what he had left over, but with his all. Are
we not called to follow the example of Saint Joseph
in our own lives?

— Marianne Patrovito

WHO CAN YOU lovingly serve this day? Are you giving out of your "leftovers," or offering all you have
in love?

*Prayer: Saint Joseph, may I follow your example of selfless
love in action. Amen.*

December 31

Learn to do good;
seek justice,
correct oppression;
defend the fatherless. — Isaiah 1:17

A protector guards the body, the mind, the emotions, and the spirit. Protecting the body includes avoiding physical harm as well as modeling chastity and healthy choices. Protecting the mind includes ensuring positivity and hope outweigh the negative. Protecting emotions involves affirming another's self-worth. Protecting the spirit comes through practicing faith in a way that encourages prayer, consideration, openness, and love.

Joseph had the DNA of a protector. He intended to protect Mary's dignity even when planning to divorce her. By accepting her as his wife, he protected her faith, her feelings, and her physical well-being. Joseph protected his family from physical harm by fleeing to safety. Joseph's complete trust in God also helped to protect Jesus' and Mary's faith.

— Tracey Reid

WITH WHOM can I share my faith today in a way that will make them feel protected and respected?

Prayer: Joseph, your faith gave you the strength and courage to protect and guide your family. Help me to strengthen my faith to become a humble protector. Amen.

January 1, Mary Mother of God

The LORD passed before him, and proclaimed, "The LORD, the LORD, a God merciful and gracious, slow to anger, and abounding in mercy and faithfulness, keeping merciful love for the thousands." — Exodus 34:6–7

Love is the deepest desire and need of the human heart. There is affectionate love, romantic love, enduring love, familiar love, self-love, selfless love, sacrificial love. But the love of a father is singular, formative, protective. Fathers instill a sense of safety, well-being, security, and protection. They emulate God as our first protector. Joseph is all these things.

I try to imagine what went through the mind and heart of Joseph as his life unfolded with this call to be a husband to Mary and a father to her child. As a devout Jewish man, perhaps his heart recalled this verse from Exodus. It would have been impossible for Joseph to walk the journey with the unfailing trust, faithfulness, and courage if he did not know that love is God's name. Joseph knew that his Father in heaven was with him, loving him and his family.

— Colleen Case

WHERE DO YOU need God's protection? Where do you need the love of the Father in your life?

Prayer: Blessed Saint Joseph, help us grow to know and trust in God's protecting and providential love for us. Amen.

January 2

Let love be genuine; hate what is evil, hold fast to what is good; love one another with brotherly affection; outdo one another in showing honor. — *Romans 12:9–10*

Joseph appears to have been a humble and quiet man with a great capacity to love. He was entrusted by God to love, nurture, and protect a small life, enabling the child to fly into his own purpose and glory. Joseph had the benefit of knowing that Jesus was bound for great things and had faith in Jesus to make the right decisions on the journey.

Often, parents think of a child as "mine." Joseph understood from the beginning that Jesus was not "his," but that God had entrusted his Son to him. Yet Joseph loved Jesus sincerely. He devoted his life to preparing the child for a bigger calling, a mission he did not live long enough to see unfold. I envision Joseph hugging Jesus daily, quietly imparting wisdom or teaching, and trusting that the fruits of Jesus' life would fulfill the Father's will.

— Tracey Reid

WHAT WOULD our world be like if every parent could look at their child as God's own child entrusted to them? How can you do this in your own life?

Prayer: Joseph, humble, quiet, loving father, help me to hold onto all that is good. Amen.

January 3

Let not loyalty and faithfulness forsake you;
bind them about your neck,
write them on the tablet of your heart. — Proverbs 3:3

For Joseph, the virtues of love and fidelity were inseparable, forming an unbreakable bond of devotion to the Lord and Mary. It was his love and fidelity that helped Joseph decide to follow the Lord's command to take Mary into his home. Many men in his situation would have walked away. But Joseph, a holy man of God, remained steadfast. His fidelity to Mary never wavered, bound by love. While Joseph may not have understood the situation nor the circumstances, he ultimately and freely chose to remain by her side, for his beloved's name was written on Joseph's heart.

Married couples today can learn a great deal from the loving relationship of Mary and Joseph. The life they shared together was not without hardships and heartbreak, yet their love for each other was unfailing because God was at the center of the love.

— Dr. Mary Amore

REFLECT ON your relationship with those you love. How can Joseph's life inspire you to deepen your commitment to be loving and faithful?

Prayer: Saint Joseph, beloved spouse of Mary, help me to renew my love and faith to God and to my family. Amen.

January 4

Fear not, for I am with you,
be not dismayed, for I am your God;
I will strengthen you, I will help you,
I will uphold you with my victorious right hand.
— Isaiah 41:10

Have you ever turned to Saint Joseph for protection? When I have felt alone and lost, I have looked to Joseph for protection and direction. Like a vulnerable child, I have placed my trust and power in the hands of not only my heavenly Father, but also Saint Joseph, the foster father of us all.

Breathe in this truth: Saint Joseph's participation in God's Fatherhood extends to all of us. Joseph is here to guide us in times of trouble, to comfort us when we hurt, and to protect us from the evil one. He extends to all the love with which he guided and guarded Christ himself. There is no need to look for someone who will make us feel safe and secure; God has already assigned that role to Saint Joseph.

— Lori Bertucci-Thibeau

TAKE TIME to meditate on Saint Joseph. Rest in his fatherly protection. Saint Joseph loved God with all his heart, and he loves us, too, and will watch over us always.

Prayer: Saint Joseph, we thank you for watching over us and keeping us safe. Help us to grow in faith. Amen.

January 5

On these two commandments depend all the law and the prophets. — Matthew 22:40

All the Gospel stories involving Joseph support the notion that he loved God, Mary, Jesus, and his neighbor. When I think of the commandments to love God above all and love your neighbor as yourself, I reword it just a little. I say, "Love God by loving your neighbor."

The self-sacrificing love we see in Joseph's life as portrayed in Scripture can be a model for us. We can begin by loving those near and dear to us, and then we can expand beyond that. Loving your neighbor can sometimes be quite a challenge. Simple acts of love are always possible while we are standing in a line at the store, driving, stopped at a red light, or whenever we encounter a stranger. Volunteering at a food pantry, a homeless shelter, or a retirement home are all ways of stepping out of our comfort zone and imitating Joseph as we love our neighbors as ourselves in an ever-enlarging circle.

— Bob Frazee

How can you serve your neighbor today?

Prayer: Beloved Saint Joseph, pray for me as I strive to love the Lord and my neighbor as myself. Amen.

January 6

The LORD, your God, is in your midst,
a warrior who gives victory;
he will rejoice over you with gladness,
he will renew you in his love. — Zephaniah 3:17

We all need to feel safe and protected. God always guards us with the power of his protection, yet we sometimes need to be reminded that he remains in our midst and constantly watches over us.

Joseph is our protector, too. Responsible for the protection of the Holy Family while he lived, from the spiritual realm Joseph is now protects of the Mystical Body of Christ. He is guardian of the universal Church, shielding the family of God from evil. Joseph is a warrior and intercessor who protects us and leads us to safety in the arms of God.

— Nanci Lukasik-Smith

HAVE YOU EVER experienced a time when you needed protection from someone? Did you find the protection you needed? Have you ever protected someone else from danger?

Prayer: Holy Saint Joseph, protector of the Divine and of humanity, I ask you to place your shield of strength and protection over our families, and guide them away from evil. Help us to become holy as we live our faith, safe in the arms of the God who loves us. Amen.

About the Contributors

Dr. Mary Amore holds a Doctor of Ministry Degree in Liturgical Studies and a Master of Arts in Pastoral Studies from Catholic Theological Union. A published author and national presenter, Dr. Amore is the editor and co-contributor of *Every Day with Mary*. Married, the mother of two adult children and grandmother of two grandchildren, Dr. Amore currently serves as the full-time executive director of Mayslake Ministries.

Dr. Jill Bates holds degrees from DePaul University, Loyola University, and a Doctor of Ministry from The Graduate Theological Foundation. Jill has worked in the areas of adult faith formation, ecumenism, and chaplaincy. Led by the Holy Spirit and nourished in the community, she finds personal enrichment in her current role as spiritual director at Mayslake Ministries.

Amy Bovie is a wife, mom, grandma, sister, friend, teacher, spiritual director, retreat leader, public speaker, published author, and faithful lover of Christ. An avid gardener and cook, Amy helps others see the beauty-goodness of God in themselves, others, and the world around us, so they can share the Good News with others. Amy serves as a spiritual director at Mayslake Ministries.

Meg Bucaro is a professional speaker, communications skills expert, Mom to three energetic kiddos and wife to one amazing husband. She works with women who desire to increase credibility, likability, and influence through their communication behaviors. Meg also speaks to Catholic women about living with more soul-filling peace (and a little humor) during the highs and lows of motherhood. Meg is part of the Mayslake Ministries Women's Ministry.

Colleen Case is associate director of the Office of Youth Formation directing Teen Formation and Confirmation with the Diocese of Joliet. She studied chemistry, philosophy, and psychology at the University of Illinois, Chicago. She is a spiritual director with Mayslake Ministries and an instructor in their Sacred Presence - Spiritual Directors Certification Program. Her passion for youth and young adults, along with her zeal for sharing the love of Jesus and his Church, has led her to numerous speaking and media projects. Colleen and her husband currently reside in the Chicagoland, spending their free time enjoying their amazing young adult children.

Denine Chambers is a certified spiritual director and self-published poet. She is passionate about her faith, family, and friends. Denine enjoys her involvement in presenting retreats, serving in many ministries, and helping others to encounter Christ. She finds joy in listening to the heart stories of others, seeing God in all things, and helping others to do the same. Denine serves as a spiritual director for Mayslake Ministries.

Larry Dreffein is a teacher, pastor, and administrator following the call of the Gospel in the footsteps of Saint Francis of Assisi for the last fifty years. An accomplished spiritual director at Mayslake Ministries and facilitator in the Mayslake Ministries Sacred Presence Program, he has accompanied many on their journey, listening to the call placed in their lives and helping them discern its meaning and direction.

Bob Frazee holds a Master's in Pastoral Studies from Catholic Theological Union - Chicago. His passion is adult spiritual formation. He has served as an RCIA catechist, an instructor in the Joliet Diocesan Lay Formation program, and as an adjunct to the Emmaus Program at CTU. Bob is an affiliate of Mayslake Ministries, and the director of the Mayslake Sacred Presence Program for the formation of spiritual directors. He also serves as a commissioned presenter for Contemplative Outreach where he promotes and teaches centering prayer.

Mary Lally obtained her training as a spiritual director through The Christos Center "Tending the Holy" program. A registered nurse, Mary holds a Master's of Public Health with a focus in Health Education. Her experience includes eighteen years of community work, while employed at the DuPage County Health Department. She is a Healing Touch Practitioner, using "healing prayer" as the basis for her practice. She believes that everyone has a unique spiritual journey and story to unravel. Mary serves Mayslake Ministries as a spiritual director.

JoAnne McElroy, MA, holds a Master of Arts in contemporary spirituality and a post-graduate certificate in spiritual direction from the Institute of Pastoral Studies at Loyola University of Chicago. JoAnne takes a contemplative approach to spiritual direction, incorporating the arts and nature. She is a commissioned presenter of centering prayer. JoAnne loves exploring nature with her husband, children, and grandchildren.

Dr. Elizabeth McGovern has a PhD in Archaeology and the His- tory of Art, specializing in the cultures of ancient Egypt and Medieval Europe. Her research addresses how clothing and self-presentation communicate information about identity, both individual and communal. She is a wife and the mother of two young daughters and is an adjunct lecturer at New York University and a guest presenter at the Mayslake Ministries Women's Teas.

Sr. Mary McNulty is a Sisinawa Dominica and has been involved in teaching and adult faith formation in parishes in the Chicagoland area. Sr. Mary serves as a spiritual director for Mayslake Ministries.

Kathy Micheli holds a Master of Arts in Pastoral Ministry from St. Joseph College in Maine. She is an affiliate spiritual director at Mayslake Ministries where she received her certification in spiritual direction and holds a Bachelor of Music in Education from DePaul. A retired piano and early childhood music instructor, Kathy has worked as a catechist, music minister, and is currently preserving stories of faith through spiritual writing.

Lauren Nelson is married and the mother of two young girls. She holds a Bachelor of Arts in Theology and is a co-contributing author to *Every Day with Mary*. Lauren serves as the assistant director of religious education at a Catholic Parish in the Diocese of Joliet. A frequent presenter in the Women's Ministry at Mayslake Ministries, Lauren enjoys sharing her love of the Catholic Faith with others.

Maria Pusateri holds a certificate in spiritual direction through Mayslake Ministries and a certificate in lay leadership through the Diocese of Joliet. She has worked in various parish ministries for over twenty years. As a wife and mother of three young adult children she has a heart for Marian spirituality. Maria is currently pursuing a degree in theology through Franciscan University of Steubenville.

Tracey Reid is a certified spiritual director with Mayslake Ministries. A program management director by profession, Tracey holds a Bachelor's in Computer Science and a Master's in Information Systems Management and Security. With a NewWine certification in lay ministry, Tracey served several years in faith development, youth catechism, and education leadership. Her current ministry is teaching computers and technology to those needing skills for employment. Her passion is open discourse on faith, the Spirit, and life that thrives within the unknowing.

Sue Rooney has a background in microbiology and medical technology. She holds a Master of Arts in Pastoral Studies from Loyola University Chicago and has worked as a chaplain. Sue is passionate about the connection between medicine and spirituality. She currently serves others as a spiritual director with Mayslake Ministries.

Gina Sannasardo, EdM, is married and is the mother of two beautiful children. A teacher/catechist of over fifteen years, Gina serves as the assistant principal of a Catholic school in the Diocese of Joliet. Gina has a strong faith and has seen God's miraculous love and mercy interwoven into her everyday life. Gina is part of the Mom's Ministry Team at Mayslake Ministries.

Carol Schubert, CPSD, is a former youth minister. She currently serves as adult faith formation and liturgy director at a Catholic Parish in the Diocese of Joliet. Carol holds a BA in Pastoral Ministry from Dominican University and is a certified professional spiritual director with Mayslake Ministries.

Alice Smith holds a Master's of Science in Home Economics Education. Her ministry — "What's New with You and Jesus" — examines family life in relationship to Jesus, weaving Scripture and prayer into family stories resulting in a spiritual legacy. Alice is a member of the board of directors of Mayslake Ministries and assists the executive director with matters concerning the board.

Nanci Lukasik-Smith, CPSD, is a co-contributing author of *Every Day with Mary*. Nanci holds a certificate of study in lay leadership through the University of St. Mary of the Lake in Mundelein, Illinois; an advanced certificate in special needs faith formation from the University of Dayton (VLCFF); and is currently a candidate for a Master's in Pastoral Studies. She completed the Life-Coach training program through Catholic Theological Union, with a focus on working with those in ministry and church administration. Nanci serves as a spiritual director for Mayslake Ministries.

Deacon Jerry Souta Jr. is a permanent deacon at a Catholic parish in the Archdiocese of Chicago. Deacon Jerry is married and serves as a spiritual director for Mayslake Ministries.

Lori Bertucci-Thibeau is a pastoral counselor and certified spiritual director since 2015, specializing in Ignatian and Carmelite spiritualities, trauma, women's issues, and contemplative prayer. Her practice includes men and women dealing with the "dark night," prayer, relationships, and family life. She is committed to journeying with clients in discovering the movements of God in the individual's walk of faith. As a pastoral counselor, Lori has facilitated the development of parish ministries and programs across Chicagoland. Married, a mother and grandmother, Lori serves Mayslake Ministries as a spiritual director.